FIGHTERS, REFUGEES, IMMIGRANTS

To my wife, Audrey, and our children, Lynn, Alan, Pam,
and Betsy, whose love and thoughts were always with me;
To my partners, who were so willing to take
on more work in my absence;
To Stan Breen and the American Refugee Committee and
to Dr. Karen Olness, who said, "Do it!"
To DeAnn Rice and Karen Turnquist, my most competent and
compassionate colleagues and my very good friends;
And to the Hmong, with gratitude and hope for the future.

Manufactured in the United States of America

Designed by Gale Houdek

LIBRARY OF CONGRESS CATALOGING IN PUBLICATION DATA

Goldfarb, Mace.
  Fighters, refugees, immigrants.

    1. Refugees—Thailand—Case studies.
  2. Hmong (Asian people)—Thailand—Case studies.
  I. Title.
  HV640.4.T5G63   306′.0899591   82-4370
  ISBN 0-87614-197-1   AACR2

        2 3 4 5 6 7 8 9 10 87 86 85 84 83

FIGHTERS, REFUGEES, IMMIGRANTS
A story of the Hmong

by Mace Goldfarb, M.D.

Carolrhoda Books, Inc., Minneapolis

AUTHOR'S NOTE

People have asked me why I, an American pediatrician living a comfortable life with the best medical equipment and knowledge available to me, decided to volunteer to work in an Indochinese refugee camp in Thailand. There were many reasons, but when I look back on it now, two stand out above the others.

The first is fairly simple. The chance to use my skills where they would really make a difference was important to me. A doctor in the United States helps people, certainly, but most of my patients would live without that help. Since there are thousands of doctors to choose from, one individual doesn't usually make that big a difference. But in a refugee camp that's not the case. Doctors are few, and they can and do save lives.

The second reason has to do with my sense of my own history. I suppose that at one time or another almost everybody's ancestors were refugees. But mine were refugees in the more recent past, and so perhaps my emotional connections with refugees today are more immediate. It seemed to me that I had no right to complain that the refugees in my family had been treated poorly if I were not willing to help today's refugees.

Nevertheless, when I first decided to go to Thailand, I thought of Southeast Asia as little more than a small piece of land below China. As for the refugees themselves, I thought of them simply as people to be pitied. I imagined they pitied themselves as well. How wrong I was!

I have tried in this book to give a picture of life at a particular Thai refugee camp, Ban Vinai, amidst a particular refugee people, the Hmong. It is by no means a complete picture, and it reflects only my own experience. If any generalizations are to be drawn, you, the reader, will have to draw them. One of the lessons I learned at Ban Vinai was that generalizing, at least for me, is a risky business.

HISTORICAL NOTE

Situated in northeastern Thailand nine miles from the Mekong River, Ban Vinai Refugee Camp was originally set up in 1975 to help the earliest refugees from the Communist takeover of Laos. Most of these refugees were the leaders of a people who called themselves the Hmong (moohng). They had come from high in the Laotian mountains where they had been farmers who also raised livestock.

The Hmong had not always been mountain people. Since they have no written language, no one is certain where they came from originally. We do know that at one time they were lowland rice farmers in China, but they were pushed into the mountains by invaders. About 150 years ago some of them began to move from southern China into Southeast Asia, where they settled in the mountains of Thailand, Vietnam, and Laos.

The Hmong have long been known for their fierce independence. Their name for themselves means "free man." (The Laotians call them Meo [MAY-oh], which means "barbarians.") When the French, who controlled Indochina in the 1890s, imposed what the Hmong felt was an unfair tax, the Hmong fought them. This war lasted about twenty years. There followed about thirty years of peace. Then the Japanese invaded the area in 1941, during World War II. The Hmong went to war against the Japanese, this time allied with France and other nations, and gained a reputation as excellent guerrilla fighters. In the early 1960s this reputation led the Americans to ask the Hmong for help in a war that the United States was then fighting against the Communists in Vietnam.

The Hmong agreed to fight for the United States during the Vietnam War, and they fought hard and well. Their casualties were terrible—as much as 100 times the rate of American casualties—and by the end of the war even Hmong children were being recruited. There are many stories of twelve-year-old Hmong boys going off to fight.

When the United States left Indochina and the Vietnamese and Laotian governments came under Communist control, the Hmong were left without allies in the midst of their enemies. Having fought against them for fourteen years, the Hmong were now hated by the Communists, who proceeded to bomb and gas Hmong villages. The Hmong had no choice but to flee.

What do you think of when you think of a refugee camp? Groups of people sitting around with their heads in their hands looking sad? That's pretty much what I had expected. I couldn't have been more wrong!

I arrived at Ban Vinai Refugee Camp, where I had volunteered my services as a doctor, in October of 1979. What I found was a bustling marketplace. There were tailor shops, restaurants, barbershops, even a dentist. People were farming, buying and selling goods, and playing soccer and volleyball in the evenings. I was astonished.

Most of the refugees at Ban Vinai are Hmong. They had little choice about leaving their homes in the mountains of Laos. Their enemies now control the Laotian government, and from all reports, that government seems determined to wipe out the Hmong. Their villages have been bombed, napalmed, and gassed, so for the Hmong it is either leave home or die.

Everyone goes. Old people, babies, mothers, young men trek through the jungle trying to avoid patrols and mines, then cross the wide and sometimes deep Mekong River which makes up the border between Laos and Thailand. It is a journey fraught with danger, and some reports indicate that as many as one out of every two Hmong die along the way. Since they must cross the river in groups, they are much more visible to border patrols than they would be if alone, and many are killed at this last stage of their journey. Some make it across only to be turned back by Thai border guards.

If all goes well, when the refugees cross the Mekong they are picked up by Thai police and taken to a transient camp where they are housed in lean-tos and given some clothes, kitchen utensils, and food. But I heard many stories in Ban Vinai of Hmong who were beaten and raped before they arrived at the transient camp. I also heard stories of Thai villagers who would not allow the Hmong to cross the river unless they could pay many thousand Baht (rhymes with lot) to the village. (One Baht = $.05)

A doctor speaks to a group of Hmong refugees who have just arrived at the transient camp.

After a few weeks at the transient camp, the refugees are brought into the main camp at Ban Vinai. They immediately seek out their relatives, who assist them in obtaining food and getting settled.

The Hmong at Ban Vinai are well organized. They are divided into about twenty family clans. One chief is in overall charge. Below him are several sub-chiefs who are in charge of smaller groups.

This system made it much easier for medical workers to organize things like immunizations. We convinced the Hmong chief, he told the heads of the smaller groups, and they in turn made sure that everyone showed up for the shots.

About two weeks after I arrived at camp, we were told of a case of diptheria. I immediately went to the chief who quickly arranged for me to examine the people who might have been infected. He did this by passing the word through his chain of command. The Hmong's close family ties and their military experience make this kind of communication very efficient.

The Ban Vinai Camp Director and a
public health nurse discuss an issue
with the Hmong chief. The last build-
ing on the road behind them housed
many of the medical personnel.

When Ban Vinai was originally established in 1975, it was intended to hold about 12,000 refugees. But as the Communist regime in Laos grew stronger and began to step up attacks and harrassment of the Hmong, more and more Hmong were forced to flee. By July of 1979 the camp population had jumped from 12,000 to 42,000.

Housing at Ban Vinai has been built in stages as more people have arrived and as more money has become available. In the beginning, houses were made of bamboo and thatch with earthen floors. This allowed air—and insects— free movement. Bamboo and thatch houses were what the Hmong had built in Laos. Later houses were built out of metal and sat on posts above the ground. While I was there, the new houses were being made of concrete with metal roofs and looked like they would be very hot.

Large families live together in one house. To the Hmong, family is of supreme importance. "To be with family is to be happy," they say. "To be without family is to be lost." The women outnumber the men, and the Hmong are polygamous. A man might have two or three wives or more—as many as he can support. He and his wives, their young children, their grown sons, and their sons' families all share the same quarters. My interpreter and his family lived with his father and twenty-four other family members. They had one large room for living, cooking, and eating, and three small bedrooms just big enough for mats and bedrolls.

Above: Early thatch and bamboo housing at Ban Vinai, built to stay cool, but unfortunately ideal for insects and rodents as well as for people. Below: A typical street scene in Ban Vinai. Grandparents often care for young children while parents work.

Water in Ban Vinai is scarce. It is pumped from five or six
deep wells and many shallow wells, then stored in tanks
about two stories high.

Drinking water is boiled and often colored with tea to
mark it as drinkable. It is available for only three or four
hours each day. To obtain it, people wait in line for long
periods of time and carry it long distances.

Left: Refugees and pails lined up at the water tanks. The pails hold people's places in line. Right: A mother bathes her healthy child and her sick child outside the pediatric ward a few feet from the water tanks. Parents spend a great deal of time with their hospitalized children, tending to whatever needs don't require a doctor or nurse. The importance of this kind of family care in hospitals is something we are just now learning about in the U.S.

Bathing water is available from large forty-gallon jugs near the storage tanks. People bathe by dipping a container into the jug and pouring the water over themselves—a cold but refreshing shower. I enjoyed it until I began to think of the number of trips the little girl responsible for filling the jugs had to make between them and the tanks so that I might shower. Bathing is also done in the nearby lake.

Refugees in line for milk and biscuits, distributed twice a day to children and pregnant women by "Food for the Hungry," a world organization.

The food at Ban Vinai is the food of poor people all over the world—stew. Everything is boiled in water—vegetables and chicken or fish—then served with rice. The hot water prevents bacterial growth and fills the stomach.

As in most societies, eating at Ban Vinai is a very social activity. Usually the men eat together. The women who serve them eat later with the children. On festive occasions I saw the women sit down with the men, but they still did all the preparing and serving.

Most of the food available is paid for by the United Nations and delivered to the camp by Thai merchants. Its distribution amazed me. Long lines of people waited patiently while one of their leaders weighed and distributed relatively small amounts of rice, vegetables, and meat or fish. For most of the people in line this would be the total supply of food for three days, yet there was never the pushing or shoving I have seen in the U.S. for items of far less importance.

Additional food—grown or raised in the camp or brought in by Thai traders—can be bought in one of Ban Vinai's four or five markets. Ducks, chickens, vegetables, home-made tofu, sweets, and soda pop are all available. I particularly liked a noodle shop that specialized in a delicious soup made with noodles, vegetables, pork, and spices.

Of course, to buy food people need money. The money at Ban Vinai is in the form of Baht, which is the currency of Thailand. Some Baht is undoubtedly brought across the Mekong with the refugees, some is sent by relatives in a better position, and some is earned from work done in camp. Most refugees, however, don't have money.

Besides food the markets sell household goods, cassette tapes, even Western medicines. My curiosity drew me to the Western medicine shop where all kinds and colors of pills and capsules were sold. Of course, in a refugee market no one needs a doctor's prescription. People would just buy handfuls of different-colored pills. Never mind that these pills all had different—and sometimes opposite— effects! This created a real problem in the medical clinics and hospitals since a patient might very likely have been taking the wrong drug for his or her disease.

Everybody loves ice cream! Here in one of the markets is a Thai ice cream truck.

Taking medicines for disease is not new to the Hmong.
They have used plants as medicines for centuries, and
Western medicines have been available to them since the
Vietnam War. When the American army came into Hmong
villages during the war, they brought large amounts of
Western medicines with them; unfortunately they did not
bring the Hmong any knowledge of how to use those
medicines.

The Hmong believe strongly in spirits, or animism. They
feel that disease occurs when the spirit leaves the body,
and that diseases are cured when the spirit has been
enticed to return. When I first came to Ban Vinai, I
wondered about the peculiar markers I saw around the
camp. They were signposts to lure back various people's
spirits. As a Western "medicine man," I was impressed
with how well this animism worked for many patients
with psychological or psychosomatic diseases.

A woman selling herbs she has grown
and dried. Some of these herbs are
probably love potions, others are
medicines for various diseases.

Left: A grandmother in front of the family garden she helps tend. Right: Refugees have made poor plots of land behind the camp bloom with peppers, beans, okra, and other vegetables. Refugees pay rent to the Thai for the land.

Being a refugee and leaving home also means leaving behind many old ways. What employment is there in a refugee camp? Most of the men had been farmers and, more recently, soldiers. The women had worked in their homes, tended gardens, sold goods in the markets, and done some needlework. Their work in the camp is essentially the same, but the men have no steady employment. A few work for the agency running the camp. Others have small plots of land outside the camp that they farm. But because of the ever increasing number of refugees, no more land is available for rent. Some men are able to begin businesses as tailors, blacksmiths, and barbers, providing services needed by this community of 42,000. But the large proportion of men are forced to be idle—a condition they despise.

A teacher writes on the blackboard in a classroom. Families must pay for their children to go to school.

Schools for the young are also a problem. The children are eager to learn. They are especially interested in English classes since many of them want to come to the United States. But children begin to work at an early age in Laos—and in Ban Vinai. Eight-year-old girls watch the younger children and haul water and food. Boys also help with the household chores and with any garden work that needs to be done. But many of them go to school even though it is not well organized or compulsory.

There was a solid group of educated refugees in the camp when I arrived. They had been educated in Laos and, because of their work with the Americans during the Vietnam War, had learned basic English. Most of the interpreters and teachers came from this group.

Children begin to work at an early age. This girl is carrying water to her family's garden. The mounds on the road serve as stepping stones during the rainy season.

Thailand is a tropical country. I therefore expected to see tropical diseases and indeed I did—diseases I had only read about in medical books in the U.S. But the primary diseases of Ban Vinai are less a result of the tropics than a result of the close living and the filth and squalor inherent in a refugee camp. Tuberculosis, malaria, pneumonia, diarrhea, and skin infections are unavoidable in these conditions. I treated many cases of tuberculosis on the pediatric ward.

My first week there was one I'll never forget. Here in the U.S. my patients are mostly well or mildly ill children with only an occasional critically ill child. There I was faced immediately with twenty seriously ill and several dying children, and more came every day.

I have often heard the attitude expressed in the U.S. that "Life is cheap in Asia." Nothing could be further from the truth! I remember one three-year-old girl who was very ill with tuberculosis. She had haunting eyes and a body withered from the disease. Her father was with her constantly, encouraging her to eat, playing games with her, and pleading with me to save his child when it was obvious to all that she was dying.

When he accepted her approaching death, he brought the other children in one by one to say a final good-bye. When she died, both parents began to wail and grieve. Her father tenderly picked up her wasted body in his arms, then gathered up the pots and meager belongings that had been next to her bed. Those that had been the child's toys would be placed on top of her grave.

Pao Fang was a ten-year-old orphan boy with tuberculosis. I can still see him, ribs with no flesh, standing in
front of the hospital looking curious. He belonged inside,
not outside. Karen, a nurse anesthetist from Minneapolis,
took him under her motherly wing. I gave him the proper
medicine; she gave him love, extra clothes, and a lot of
food. He gained ten pounds in two weeks and was clearly
getting better.

Pao Fang on his way to good health.
He's obviously enjoying his meal.

Above Left: His healthy sister visits a boy sick with anemia and what we then diagnosed as tuberculosis but could well have been the effects of chemical warfare. The evidence we have now clearly indicates that Hmong villages were subjected to chemical attacks, but while I was at Ban Vinai this evidence was just coming to light. Above Right: When I saw this mother leaving the hospital with her very sick child, I was terrified that she was taking him home. (Parents sometimes did take their children home at night.) I raced after her and was relieved to discover, after a series of somewhat comic gestures, that she was only helping him go to the bathroom. Right: The pediatric ward.

The hospital was a series of barracks-like buildings. Inside were rows of hard wooden pallets with wicker mats. There was a small lab with little equipment and a delivery room—and that was it. X-rays and lab tests were often impossible to obtain. Making an accurate diagnosis was sometimes difficult, to say the least!

Add to that the complication of having to use an interpreter. It was a new experience for me to speak through another person to a mother who couldn't understand what I was saying. She in turn was trying to tell me about a third person—my patient, her child. I had to take care to speak slowly, to use different ways of expressing the same idea, and not to use slang. I learned to watch faces and gestures more than I ever had before.

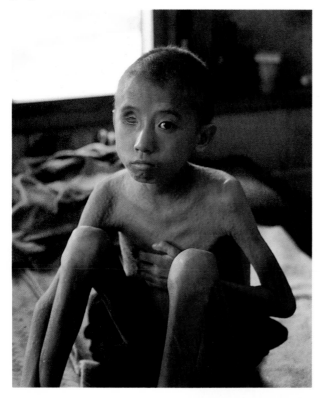

Left: This boy is not suffering from malnutrition but from chronic disease and scabies, a severe, infectious skin disease. He lost his eye as a result of being shot by a Laotian. Below: One of our favorite patients dressed for warm weather...and cold. His necklaces and bracelets are good luck charms.

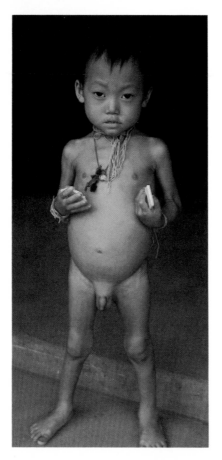

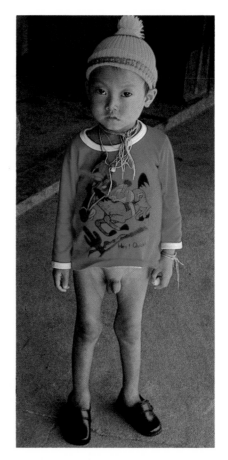

During my first weekend at Ban Vinai I decided to stay in camp in case of any emergencies and to avoid the long two-hour ride each way to Loei, the nearest large town. I was surprised that weekend to see the vibrancy of life in camp. Hundreds crowded around the court to watch young men play volleyball. That afternoon the Hmong team beat the local Thai village team. There was a lot of cheering and groaning over missed shots. Later in the evening families came out for a stroll near the athletic field. Young boys spun their tops with long cords. Older boys played soccer and a kind of football. Life suddenly seemed like fun that Saturday. I had needed to get away from the sickness for a time, and the Hmong needed relief from the immediate squalor around them.

Several weeks later a group of us (doctors and nurses) challenged a Hmong volleyball team. We lost miserably, but in doing so provided much laughter for the onlookers.

What an incredible experience the time I spent at Ban Vinai was for me! I gave so small a measure of my help and gained so much from these refugees as persons. (I use the word "persons" because you never meet "a people," only individuals.) World events have since seemed more real; newspapers now speak to me of individuals, not just numbers.

Where do the Hmong go from Ban Vinai and what happens to them? About four out of five ask to come to the United States, but they must be approved by American immigration authorities first and there can be problems. The Hmong practice of polygamy is just one. Perfectly acceptable in Laos, polygamy is not accepted in the United States. Since a man is allowed to bring only one wife, families must be broken up in order for some family members to immigrate to the U.S. Considering their reverence for family, this is very difficult for the Hmong.

Those who do immigrate are faced with new problems. There are thousands of strange new things to be learned: how to read prices at a store, how to handle a checking or savings account at a bank, how to use a telephone. The men are faced with particularly difficult problems. A man who was a powerful leader in Laos becomes an illiterate immigrant upon arrival in the United States. His skills in farming and guerrilla warfare don't transfer, so what is he to do for work? How is he to support his family and maintain the prestige he formerly enjoyed in his community? His problem is made more complicated by the experiences of other family members. His children are in school learning English and acclimating to this new culture. His wife's homemaking skills *do* transfer and, in addition, Hmong women are excited to find new freedoms for themselves in the U.S. It is a difficult situation for Hmong men and some of them talk of going back to their homeland to fight against the government in Laos.

Above Left: Children in the transient camp. Above Right: A mother and her child dressed for the Hmong New Year. The New Year celebration lasts for about a week and is the most important holiday in the Hmong year. Below Left: A woman holding a digging tool in front of the gardens. Of course, all garden work is done by hand. Below Right: Mother sews while Father tends their newborn baby.

Hmong women selling their beautiful hand-made tapestries in a market. On this particular day, U.S. governors were touring the camp, so sales were probably particularly good.

Hmong who have immigrated to the U.S. continue to make these exquisite tapestries which have been exhibited in several museums and art shows. They are not only a source of income to the U.S. Hmong, but a source of great pride as well.

But it's not unusual for the first generation of immigrants to have one foot in their country of origin and another foot in their adopted country. The second generation will no doubt have stronger feelings toward *their* United States. In the meantime, I truly believe that the qualities I witnessed in these remarkable people at Ban Vinai will see them through. Though I had expected to find the refugees bemoaning the tragic circumstances that had befallen them, their spirit, vitality, and enthusiasm overtook me. Their strong sense of family and community supported each individual, and there is no doubt in my mind that this family support is being brought here with them to the United States. Many Hmong practices and attitudes are similar to American ideals. Most notably, their strong desire that their children obtain a good education is an important step toward their success. Their history of independence and willingness to work hard will serve them well too. Just as American life has been enriched by every immigrant group in the past, so will it be by the Hmong.